At the Aquarium

Volume

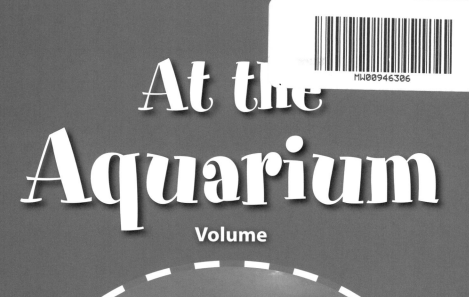

Dianne Irving

Publishing Credits

Editor
Sara Johnson

Editorial Director
Dona Herweck Rice

Editor-in-Chief
Sharon Coan, M.S.Ed.

Creative Director
Lee Aucoin

Publisher
Rachelle Cracchiolo, M.S.Ed.

Image Credits

Teacher Created Materials

5301 Oceanus Drive
Huntington Beach, CA 92649-1030
http://www.tcmpub.com
ISBN 978-0-7439-0919-8
© 2009 Teacher Created Materials Publishing

Table of Contents

Visiting an Aquarium 4

Tank Sizes 6

How Much Water? 8

Weighing the Animals 14

Feeding the Animals 22

Running an Aquarium 26

Problem-Solving Activity 28

Glossary 30

Index 31

Answer Key 32

Visiting an Aquarium

Visitors to an aquarium can see many **marine** (muh-REEN) animals. There are different kinds of fish. There are **mammals** such as whales, seals, and sea otters. And there are **invertebrates** (in-VER-tuh-bruhts) such as jellyfish and octopuses.

Marine scientists work at aquariums. They collect information about marine animals.

This marine scientist is checking tank water to test how clean it is.

A sandbar shark

Animals at an aquarium are kept in **enclosures** (in-KLOH-zhers) called tanks. Each animal needs a big enough space to live in. There are **government** (GUHV-ern-muhnt) rules about how the animals must be looked after. People who run aquariums must follow these rules. These rules protect the animals.

Tank Sizes

The size of an aquarium tank is very important. Its size and the amount of water it holds depend on the kind of animal living in the tank. The number of animals and how long they live will also affect a tank's size and amount of water.

Dolphins and seals are large marine animals. They need large tanks. These large tanks hold gallons and gallons of water. The tanks must be big enough for these animals to move around as if they were in their natural environment.

An underwater viewing tank at an aquarium

Often, tanks at aquariums are shaped like rectangular prisms. Math **formulas** are used to calculate the amount of space needed for the tanks. The formulas use **standard units** of measurement. The **volume** of tanks must be measured accurately using a standard unit—cubic feet (ft.^{3}). This is important so that the correct amount of water can be put inside the tank.

To calculate volume, multiply length by width by height: length × width × height. The tank below is 4 feet long and 2 feet wide. Its height is 2 feet. So its volume is 4ft. × 2 ft. × 2 ft. = 16 ft.^{3}

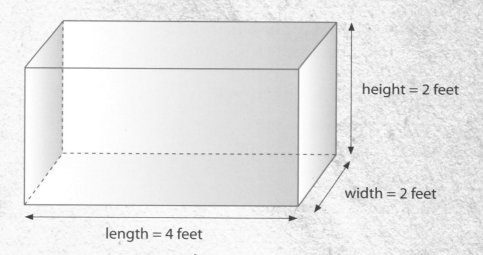

height = 2 feet

width = 2 feet

length = 4 feet

LET'S EXPLORE MATH

Use the formula for volume to answer these questions. What is the volume of a tank that is:

a. 6 feet long, 5 feet wide, and 3 feet high?

b. 12 feet long, 10 feet wide, and 4 feet high?

How Much Water?

An **average** adult beluga (buh-LOO-guh) whale is about 14 feet (4 m) in length. The length and width of a pool for just 1 beluga whale must be at least twice the length of the whale. That is 28 feet (8.5 m). The depth (height) of the tank must be at least 7 feet (2 m).

The volume of a pool this size is 5,488 cubic feet (155 m³). One cubic foot is 7.48 gallons. It takes 41,050 gallons (155,391 L) of water to fill the pool.

A beluga whale

```
     ⁶1
     28  feet (width)
  ×  28  feet (length)
    224
  + 560
    784  feet
---------------------------
     5 2
    784
  ×    7  feet (height / depth)
  5,488  cubic feet
```

The beluga whale enclosure at the Shedd Aquarium in Chicago is 18 feet (5 m) deep and holds 400,000 gallons (1.5 million L) of water. It is the largest indoor marine mammal enclosure in the world.

The Shedd Aquarium uses chemicals to make its own seawater. It takes about 3 million gallons (11.3 million L) of this seawater a year to keep the tanks filled and fresh.

LET'S EXPLORE MATH

It takes 7.48 gallons of water to fill 1 cubic foot in a tank. How much water is needed to fill:

a. a tank with a volume of 2 ft.³?

b. If a tank contains 748 gallons of water, what is the volume in cubic feet?

Sea otters often swim on their backs on the water's surface.

The average length of a sea otter is 4 feet. The length and width of a pool for just 1 sea otter must be at least 3 times the sea otter's length. The pool must be at least 3 feet (about 1 m) deep. To fill this pool, 3,231 gallons (12,230 L) of water is needed. How was this amount calculated?

LET'S EXPLORE MATH

Draw a rectangular prism to represent a tank to hold 1 sea otter. Now use the information you read above about sea otters to do the following:

a. Label the height (depth) of the tank.

b. Use the length of the sea otter to figure out the tank's length and width.

c. Figure out the volume of the tank.

How Much Water Is That?

An Olympic size swimming pool holds over 640,000 gallons (2.4 million L) of water.

The sea otter enclosure at the Monterey Bay Aquarium in California holds 55,000 gallons (208,198 L) of water. There are 4 otters living there. All the sea otters were rescued from the wild. Visitors learn about how sea otters live in the wild by watching them at the aquarium.

A sea otter enclosure

Both the width and length of a pool for just 1 seal must be at least 9 feet (2.7 m). That's about 1½ times the length of an average adult seal. The depth of the pool must be at least 3 feet (about 1 m).

The volume of a pool this size is 243 cubic feet (6.8 m^3). It will take 1,818 gallons (6,882 L) of water to fill this pool.

A harbor seal enjoying the warm sun

An aquarium worker with a beluga whale at Vancouver Aquarium

The Vancouver Aquarium in Canada has 166 displays. These displays hold a total of 2.5 million gallons (9.5 million L) of water. The aquarium is home to 4 beluga whales.

LET'S EXPLORE MATH

When you know the volume, the length, and the width of a tank, you can figure out its height. The formula to use is: Volume ÷ (length x width) = height.

The volume of the tank below is 72 ft.³ Figure out the height (depth) of the tank using the formula below and information in the diagram. *Hint*: Solve the part of the equation in the parentheses first.

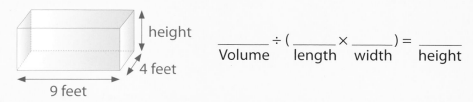

$$\underline{\quad\quad} \div (\underline{\quad\quad} \times \underline{\quad\quad}) = \underline{\quad\quad}$$
Volume   length   width   height

height

4 feet

9 feet

Weighing the Animals

Marine scientists must look after the health of the animals. Making sure the enclosures are big enough is one way of caring for the animals. Another way is to record the weight of animals to check that they are healthy.

This macaroni penguin is being weighed.

This marine scientist is weighing seal pups.

Marine scientists have information about the weights of different animal **species**. They know the usual weight of newborn and fully grown animals. Scientists use this information to check that aquarium animals are the normal weights for their ages.

Weighing Sharks

It is very difficult to weigh a shark! How would you get a shark onto a scale?

Marine scientists have come up with a formula based on measuring the weights and lengths of dead sharks. These measurements have been collected over time. Marine scientists can **estimate** the length of a shark. Then they use this information to figure out the weight of a living shark.

This grey nurse shark lives in the Melbourne Aquarium in Australia. Its tank holds over 500,000 gallons (2 million L) of water! A fully grown grey nurse shark weighs over 600 pounds (300 kg).

Tiger sharks weigh about 20 pounds (9 kg) when they are born. They weigh 850 to 1,400 pounds (386 to 635 kg) when they are fully grown.

Bonnethead sharks weigh about 6 ounces (170 g) when they are born. They weigh up to 24 pounds (11 kg) when they are fully grown.

bonnethead shark

tiger shark

Weighing Whales and Dolphins

Dolphins and baby whales can be lifted out of the water in slings. Then they can be weighed by using large **spring balances**.

When whales are fully grown, it is impossible to weigh them. They are far too big to be lifted out of the water! Instead, marine scientists estimate their lengths. Then they use a mathematical formula to estimate their weights.

Male orcas weigh around 8 tons (7,257 kg). Female orcas weigh up to 4 tons (3,629 kg).

beluga whale

bottlenose dolphins

Beluga whales weigh about 119 to 176 pounds (54 to 80 kg) when they are born. They weigh about 3,300 pounds (1,497 kg) when they are fully grown.

Atlantic bottlenose dolphins weigh about 44 pounds (20 kg) when they are born. When they are fully grown, they weigh between 440 and 660 pounds (200 to 300 kg).

LET'S EXPLORE MATH

Volume can also be measured with the metric unit of cubic meters (m^3). The formula is the same as when using cubic feet: Volume = length × width × height, but the answer is in cubic meters.

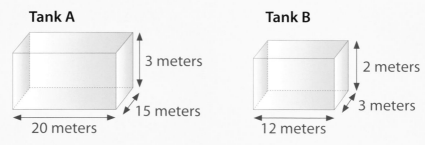

Tank A

3 meters
15 meters
20 meters

Tank B

2 meters
3 meters
12 meters

a. What is the volume of Tank A?

b. What is the volume of Tank B?

Weighing Seals, Sea Lions, and Sea Otters

Seals, sea lions, and sea otters can be trained to stand on scales. This helps marine scientists to measure their weights.

Harbor seals weigh about 22 pounds (10 kg) when they are born. They weigh 100 to 375 pounds (45 to 170 kg) when they are fully grown.

These marine scientists are weighing a sea lion.

LET'S EXPLORE MATH

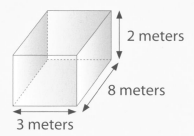

2 meters

8 meters

3 meters

In metric measurement, 1 cubic meter (1 m³) holds 1,000 liters (L) of water. Look at the tank above.

a. How many liters of water does it hold?

b. Explain how you solved this problem.

California sea lions weigh about 13 pounds (6 kg) when they are born. When they are fully grown, the females weigh 110 to 243 pounds (50 to 110 kg). Adult males weigh 440 to 880 pounds (200 to 400 kg).

Northern sea otters weigh about 3 to 5 pounds (1.4 to 2.3 kg) when they are born. When they are fully grown, the females weigh 40 to 60 pounds (18 to 27 kg). The males weigh up to 100 pounds (45 kg).

sea otter

sea lions

Feeding the Animals

It is important to give the animals the right amount of food. At aquariums, the food is carefully prepared in special kitchens. The kitchen workers weigh the food so the animals get only as much as they need.

A marine scientist preparing food

Frozen Food

Most food for aquarium animals is bought from fish suppliers. It is kept in large freezers.

This sea otter is being fed a **mollusk**.

Sea otters do not have **blubber**, as whales do, to keep them warm. They lose heat in the water. Sea otters keep warm by being active. They need to eat a lot of food for energy.

Sea otters eat about 16 pounds (7 kg) of food each day. Their diet includes mollusks such as shrimp, crab, and clams.

Beluga whales eat about 45 pounds (20 kg) of food a day. They eat squid and fish, such as herring. California sea lions eat up to 15 pounds (7 kg) of food in a day. They eat fish, squid, and octopus.

beluga whale

California sealions

Feeding dolphins

Bottlenose dolphins eat about 22 pounds (10 kg) of food a day. Their diet includes different types of fish and squid.

LET'S EXPLORE MATH

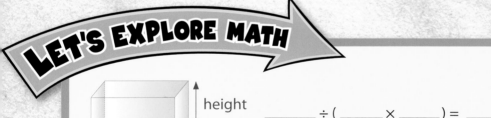

$$\underset{\text{Volume}}{\rule{1.5cm}{0.4pt}} \div (\underset{\text{length}}{\rule{1.5cm}{0.4pt}} \times \underset{\text{width}}{\rule{1.5cm}{0.4pt}}) = \underset{\text{height}}{\rule{1.5cm}{0.4pt}}$$

The volume of the tank above is 48 m³. Figure out the height (depth) of the tank using the information in the diagram and the formula: Volume ÷ (length × width) = height

Hint: Solve the part of the equation in the parentheses first.

Running an Aquarium

The Oceanarium (oh-shuh-NAIR-ee-uhm) tank at Manila Ocean Park in the Philippines holds over 3 million gallons (11.3 million L) of water. The Oceanarium features fish, sharks, rays, and marine invertebrates native to the Philippines and Southeast Asia. There is an 82 feet (25 m) long walkway tunnel through the Oceanarium.

A marine scientist inside the Oceanarium at Manila Ocean Park

This window cleaner wears **SCUBA** equipment to get the job done.

A lot of people work hard to look after the animals in an aquarium. The animals must be well fed and healthy. The tanks must be the right size and the water in the tanks must be clean. A well-maintained aquarium lets people enjoy the amazing animals that live there.

A Fishy Problem

André owns his own business. He builds both large and small tanks for aquariums. He recently built some new tanks for Seaview Aquarium.

- Tank A is 6 feet long, 4 feet wide, and 5 feet high.

- Tank B is 15 feet long, 4 feet wide, and 2 feet high.

- Tank C is 8 meters long and 4 meters wide. It has a volume of 96 cubic meters.

Solve It!

a. What are the volumes of Tanks A and B?

b. What do you notice about the volumes of both tanks?

c. What is the height of Tank C?

d. How many liters of water does Tank C hold?

Use the steps below to help you answer the questions above.

Step 1: To solve question **a**, use the formula:
length × width × height = Volume

Step 2: To answer **b**, think about the dimensions of both Tanks A and B. *Hint*: Drawing a rectangular prism for each tank and marking the dimensions may help you.

Step 3: To solve question **c**, use the formula: Volume ÷ (length × width) = height. Remember to solve the part of the equation in the parentheses first.

Step 4: Use the volume of Tank C to figure out how many liters it holds. *Hint*: 1 cubic meter (1 m³) holds 1,000 liters (L) of water.

Glossary

average—the most common or usual

blubber—a thick layer of fat under the skin of sea-dwelling mammals, such as whales and seals

enclosures—spaces for keeping animals

estimate—to judge or work out approximately

formulas—plans or strategies

government—the group of people elected to rule a country or state

invertebrates—animals without a backbone

mammals—animals whose young feed on milk from the mother

marine—living in or having to do with the sea

mollusk—an animal with a soft body that usually lives inside a shell

SCUBA—Self-Contained Underwater Breathing Apparatus

species—kinds of animals

spring balances—types of balances where weight is measured by how far the spring is stretched

standard units—common quantities or amounts that are used by most people

volume—the amount of space that an object takes up

Index

beluga whales, 8, 9, 13, 19, 24

bonnethead sharks, 17

bottlenose dolphins, 19, 25

California sea lions, 21, 24

dolphins, 6, 18–19, 25

enclosures, 5, 9, 11, 14

feeding, 22–25

formulas, 7, 13, 16, 19, 25

grey nurse shark, 16

harbor seal, 12, 20

invertebrates, 4, 26

jellyfish, 4

macaroni penguin, 14

Manila Ocean Park, 26

marine scientists, 4, 14, 15, 16, 18, 20, 22, 26

Melbourne Aquarium, 16

mollusks, 23

Monteray bay Aquarium, 11

Northern sea otters, 21

octopuses, 4

orcas, 18

rays, 26

pools, 8, 10, 12

sandbar shark, 5

scales, 16, 20

sea lions, 20, 21, 24

sea otters, 4, 10, 11, 20, 21, 23

seal pups, 15

seals, 4, 6, 12, 15, 20

seawater, 9, 23

sharks, 5, 16–17, 26

Shedd Aquarium, 9

spring balances, 18

swimming pools, 11

tanks, 4, 5, 6–7, 8, 23, 26, 27

tiger sharks, 17

Vancouver Aquarium, 13

weighing animals, 14–15, 16–17, 18–19, 20–21

whales, 4, 8, 18–19

Let's Explore Math

Page 7:

a. 6 ft. × 5 ft. × 3 ft. = 90 ft.^{3}

b. 12 ft. × 10 ft. × 4 ft. = 480 ft.^{3}

Page 9:

a. 7.48 × 2 = 14.96 gallons of water

b. Volume = 100 ft.^{3}

Page 10:

a.–b.

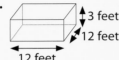

3 feet
12 feet
12 feet

c. 12 ft. × 12 ft. × 3 ft. = 432 ft.^{3}

Page 13:

Volume ÷ (length × width) = height

72 ft.^{3} ÷ (9 × 4) = height

72 ft.^{3} ÷ 36 = 2 feet high

Page 19:

a. 20 m × 15 m × 3 m = 900 m^3

b. 12 m × 3 m × 2 m = 72 m^3

Page 20:

a. 3 m x 8 m × 2 m = 48 m^3

48 m^3 × 1,000 liters = 48,000 liters of water

b. Answers will vary.

Page 25:

48 m^3 ÷ (6 m × 2 m) = height

48 m^3 ÷ 12 m = 4 meters in height

Problem-Solving Activity

a. Tank A: 6 ft. × 4 ft. × 5 ft. = 120 ft.^{3}

Tank B: 15 ft. × 4 ft. × 2 ft. = 120 ft.^{3}

b. Answers may vary, but should include the fact that Tank A and Tank B have the same volume, even though they have different dimensions.

c. 96 m^3 ÷ (8 m × 4 m) = 3 m

Tank C has a height of 3 meters.

d. 96 m^3 × 1,000 L = 96,000 L

Tank C holds 96,000 liters of water.